Family FUN

Family FUN

105 WAYS TO

- Make the most of busy days
- Bring more love and laughter into your home
- Create lasting memories
- Build family ties

Debbie Trafton O'Neal

DIMENSIONS
FOR LIVING
NASHVILLE

FAMILY FUN

Copyright © 1995 by Dimensions for Living

This book is printed on recycled, acid-free paper.

ISBN 0-687-010233
CIP data available from the Library of Congress.

The Scripture quotation on page 69 is from the New Revised Standard Version Bible, copyright © 1989, by the Division of Christian Education of the National Council of the Churches of Christ in the United States of America. Used by permission.

95 96 97 98 99 00 01 02 03 04 — 10 9 8 7 6 5 4 3 2 1

*May the celebrations of daily life
always be a part of your family fun!*

Contents

Contents

Contents

Introduction

Family time. Little else is more precious, yet families today are finding it more difficult than ever to carve time out of their busy schedules to simply have fun together. For most families, the opportunity to plan an entire day of family fun is rare, and many opportunities for making the most of the time they spend together on a daily basis are missed. There is yearning for the nostalgic feelings associated with time well spent within the family circle. How do we find time within our busy schedules to share meals, play together, and celebrate the gift of family that God has given us?

Some of the best moments families share last only a few minutes, yet these are the moments that are remembered and treasured for a lifetime. *Family Fun* is written to help families seize moments during their busy days to celebrate and enjoy being together. Whether your children are toddlers or teens, you will find fun ideas and activities within these pages that are simple and quick to plan and do. Some require a bit of preparation or preplanning, but many are perfect for those times when you have fifteen minutes and nothing to do. Grab this book at those times, but also read through it often to store up ideas to try the next time you have a few moments for family fun.

This is a book that celebrates life! As you use it within your family, you will laugh together, discover new things about each other, and most important, learn to celebrate the moments you have together. Enjoy!

CELEBRATIONS FOR ANY DAY

Celebrations for Any Day

Most families celebrate holidays and special days, but families need to celebrate their life together every day of the year. Although ideas for special days and holidays in other sections of this book can be adapted for any day, this section offers some unique ways to have fun together on ordinary days.

1. Blessings Box

You will need:

— a box
— wrapping paper and tape, or self-adhesive paper
— pieces of paper and a pen or pencil
— small objects or pictures that represent blessings, such as a toy plastic dog, a minibook, a photo of grandparents

Sometimes when we are down or having a bad day, we know that we really should be thankful and count our blessings. But this isn't always easy to do! A blessings box on the kitchen table might help.

A blessings box is something you can make quickly as a family, or you may want to prepare it ahead of time. First, remove the top of the box; decorate the box by covering it in wrapping paper or self-adhesive paper; attach a label with the words "Blessings Box."

Throughout the day, encourage family members to think about the blessings that God has given them—a pet, a brother or sister, food to eat, books to read, good health, a loving home, and so forth. Have them write their blessings on pieces of paper or find small objects or pictures to represent their blessings; then have them place the papers or objects in the box.

For a celebration on any day, reach into the blessings box and read or look at all of the blessings your family has to be thankful for. These blessings are surely something to celebrate!

2. Candlelight Dinner

You will need:

— a nice tablecloth or placemats, dishes, and table settings
— a vase of flowers or other table centerpiece
— candles and matches

Why do we always save candlelight and our best dishes and table settings for special-occasion dinners? Make mealtime special "just because"!

Set the table for your special family dinner using all of your best. Be sure to use plenty of candles to light the table. It won't matter what you serve for this meal, because being treated in this special way will make your family feel they are eating a gourmet meal!

3. Treasure Hunt

You will need:

— a piece of paper
— a candle and matches
— cold tea or coffee
— a clean paintbrush
— crayons, markers, or other writing utensils
— a treasure, such as tickets to a movie, dinner coupons, or a bag of foil-covered chocolate coins

When every day begins to have the same routine and your family needs something to give them a reason to celebrate, help them find a hidden treasure.

To make the map, carefully char the edges of a piece of paper with a candle flame so that the paper looks like an old treasure map. You might want to round the corners of the paper first so that it takes shape more quickly. Brush the charred edges off the paper and then color it by brushing cold tea or coffee over the paper. Let the paper dry; then use markers or crayons to decorate the map. Draw familiar "landmarks" in your house or yard on the map, and mark the spot where the treasure is hidden with a large X.

When you are ready, call your family together, give them the map, and let them try to find the treasure!

4. Bubble Up

You will need:

— ingredients for bubble solution:
- 3 tablespoons of glycerin (available from a drug-store)
- 3/4 cup dishwashing liquid (Joy works best)
- one gallon of distilled water (or tap water left out overnight)

— a large tub, inflatable wading pool, or plastic garbage-can lid

— bubble-making tools such as funnels, plastic clothes hangers, cookie cutters, or a wand made by tying a length of string into a loop at the end of a dowel

Any day will bubble up with excitement with this project that is fun for everyone!

Mix the bubble ingredients together and pour them into a tub or other container. Swish the bubble-making tools through the solution and see who can make the biggest bubbles! Can you see rainbows in the bubbles as they float in the sunshine?

5. Mirror Message

You will need:

— shaving cream or a foam cleanser that won't drip
— Post-it™ notes, or small slips of paper and tape
— felt-tip pens
— a hand mirror (if writing a message backward)

It is sometimes hard for today's busy families to find time to sit down and talk together. One place that everyone passes through at least once a day is the bathroom! Use the mirror in your bathroom, or a mirror in some other room in your house, as a place to leave a message.

Write a message on the mirror with shaving cream or foam cleanser. Try to find a brand that won't drip as it dries. This is especially important if the message will remain on the mirror for a long time before everyone reads it. If you choose not to use the cream or cleanser, write your message on a Post-it™ note or small slip of paper that you can tape to the mirror.

This is a great way to wish someone good luck on a test or a problem at work, but it is also a good way just to say "I love you." You might want to use this system to leave a

Bible verse, favorite saying, or inspirational thought for the day, such as "The more often I have a positive attitude, the more often I have a positive day!"

After experimenting with this type of mirror message, you might want to try writing a message on the mirror *backward*. Place a hand mirror near the message mirror to be used to read the message. (When a mirror is held in front of the backward message, it will appear correctly!)

6. Family Artwork

You will need:

— artwork
— a wall, refrigerator, or other display space
— black frames (optional)

Every family with children has a collection of artwork that is unique and that seems to multiply very quickly! You can use these art pieces in several fun and creative ways.

Family Art Gallery: Choose a space in your home to share and display all the artwork your children bring home from school or create at home. The space might be in a hallway or on the refrigerator. Or you might purchase several inexpensive black frames and hang your children's work in the living or dining room, changing the artwork periodically. And be sure to add any works of art from the older family members.

It's a Wrap: When you have an excess of artwork, don't throw it away! Use it to make book covers or to wrap gifts for others who will appreciate the time and talents of your children.

gift wrap

7. Happy Hour

You will need:

— a large piece of paper
— markers or crayons
— stickers, balloons, streamers, and other decorations
— a favorite juice, ice, glasses, and serving tray
— a munchy snack, such as pretzels
— "happy" music

Sometimes making the transition from the busyness of the day to the evening hours at home is hard for a family to do. Make a sign that says "Happy Hour" and hang it on the front door to help everyone return home with a smile.

Decorate the sign with stickers and add other decorations to the front door. Set out a tray with glasses, ice, and your favorite juice and add a bowl of pretzels or another favorite munchy snack. Play "happy" music, and let everyone relax and talk about the day before dinner or other evening activities.

8. Flashlight Hide-N-Seek

You will need:

— one working flashlight for each person

Flashlight hide-n-seek is a great game to play outside on a warm summer night. You also can play flashlight hide-n-seek in the house, but be extra careful so that no one trips and gets hurt.

The game is played in a similar fashion to regular hide-n-seek, with the players finding a hiding spot while the person who is "it" counts to 10 or 25, or whatever number you choose. Then "it" tries to shine his or her light on the players to catch them. When "it" shines the light on *you*, you're out!

Variation: The first person "it" shines a light on is the new "it."

9. Family Huddle Up

Research shows that hugging is good for you! So whenever the need arises, or when everyone is together for just a brief moment, gather together in a circle and have a group hug!

10. This Is Our Life Video

You will need:

— a video camera and videotape
— paper or posterboard and felt-tip pens

A popular television show of years past was "This Is Your Life." On the show, a guest's life was highlighted with photos and film clips of the things he or she did every day. Everyone likes to see what his or her life looks like to other people. Have fun making a video of *your* family's life!

When making silent movies years ago, they used a sign card to signal what the next scene was going to be or to provide other important information. As you and your family think about a typical day in your life, make sign cards to identify regular parts of your day or events that you want to video tape. Include key words or phrases to remind family members of specific things you want to capture on tape. Have someone hold up each sign before that particular part of the day is taped, to help family members "get ready."

Assign different people to record different parts of your family's day, focusing only on the highlights. When you have finished taping, sit back with a bowl of popcorn and enjoy watching your family on a typical day.

This is fun to do several times a year, continuing from year to year to see how everyone grows and changes.

11. The Morning Drive

You will need:

— a blank cassette tape
— a tape recorder
— favorite music, books, Bible readings, or other inspirational materials

Sometimes there is nothing more difficult than crawling into a car on a cold dark morning to begin the drive to work or school.

Make a morning-drive cassette tape to start someone's day off right. Children will enjoy helping to select and record some of the person's favorite music, a Bible reading or devotion, or passages from favorite books or reading materials. Be sure to record a special message at the beginning of the tape. On the chosen morning, slip the tape into the cassette deck of the person's car before he or she leaves. Remember to turn the cassette player on and adjust the volume, so that as soon as the person starts the car, he or she will hear a cheery message from you!

It's also fun to make tapes that children will enjoy on the way to and from school or other activities. You might even want to make special tapes for special days, such as the first and last days of school, birthdays, and holidays.

12. Cornucopia of Blessings

You will need:

— a cornucopia (perhaps wicker)
— 9 pieces of artificial or real fruit
— a Bible

We often think of the cornucopia, or "horn of plenty," as a symbol of Thanksgiving. But why use this symbol only one day or season of the year, when our lives are so full of God's blessings throughout the year?

Place the fruit in the cornucopia. Read Galatians 5:22-23 aloud together. This passage names the gifts of the Spirit, gifts that we all have but sometimes forget to acknowledge: love, joy, peace, patience, kindness, goodness, faithfulness, gentleness, and self-control. As you read, take out one piece of fruit at a time to represent each gift. For each gift, take a few moments to share with one another the times you have seen this gift from God at work in each other's lives. If you are using real fruit, enjoy eating the fruit together.

These blessings are worth celebrating every day of the year!

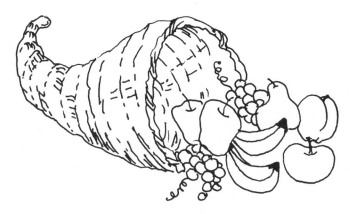

13. Tea Party

You will need:

— a pot of tea, tea cups, and a plate of cookies or small sandwiches
— a variety of hats or other dress-up clothes (for young children)

A real tea party can be a fun celebration and a time to relax and enjoy the day.

Make a pot of tea or hot cocoa and set the table for a party. Use your best china tea cups and saucers, and set a plate of cookies or small sandwiches, typical tea-party fare, in the center of the table. Small sandwiches used for tea parties are usually made of thinly sliced bread with the crusts cut off, and very simple ingredients such as thinly sliced cucumber with butter or mayonnaise, watercress and mayonnaise, or even thinly sliced meats.

Let young children choose a hat and/or dress-up clothes to wear to the tea party. Then enjoy sipping tea and talking together. There is something about sitting down for a cup of tea together that slows us down and encourages good conversation.

14. Mystery Trip

You will need:

— a map of your town or city
— money for food and events, or food or snacks to take with you

Every community has unique places to visit that many of the local residents never enjoy. Choose several of these places to visit together, without telling other members of the family where you are going—the mystery! You might take a scenic route along a road you seldom drive, stopping to look at a creek or pond along the way. Then you might go to the bowling alley for a few games, followed by a visit to a new art gallery, with a final stop at a nearby ice-cream parlor.

You and your family might like the mystery trip idea so much that you each take a turn planning a trip for other days when you want to celebrate your community and your time together as a family!

15. Family Letters

You will need:

— assorted paper and envelopes
— pens, markers, stamps, or other materials for decorating the letter
— family photos or drawings

Many families write and send a family letter to friends at Christmas, but why not use this type of communication more often?

Writing a family letter can be a project that takes as much or as little time as you have or want. Involve everyone in thinking about the type of letter you will write. Will each family member add a paragraph? Will you arrange a group of family photos on the page, and then photocopy the page? Will children's artwork form the basis of the letter? Will your letter have a seasonal theme, such as Valentine's Day or summer vacation? Will the family letter focus on a time of celebration for a special event in your life?

Type or print your letter, add photos or artwork, and then make enough photocopies to send to the people on your list. Everyone can help address the envelopes and lick the stamps. Be sure to save a copy of each letter as a record of your family activities!

16. Theme Meals

You will need:

— a favorite theme, such as dinosaurs, boating, or the study of insects
— foods that you can work with to create a "scene"
— table settings that reflect your theme, such as a colorful tablecloth, napkins, and dishes

Family members have different interests and hobbies, although they also may share a few. Why not celebrate favorite family or individual interests by having a theme meal?

This celebration meal can require preplanning, but it also can be done on the spur of the moment. After choosing your theme, decide what kinds of food will work to play out the theme. For example, mashed potatoes can be formed into volcanoes, with grated cheese melting down the sides as lava. Short pieces of broccoli can be set into the sides of the volcanoes as trees. A dinosaur cookie cutter can be used to cut turkey or ham slices into dinosaur shapes. The possibilities are endless!

17. Let's Go Fly a Kite!

You will need:

— simple store-bought kites
— permanent felt-tip pens or paints

Plan ahead for the next windy day by making simple name kites!

Help one another assemble your kites according to the directions; then decorate the kites by printing a name on each one with felt-tip pens or paints. Let dry; then store the kites until the first windy day when you can all go kite flying together!

18. Dress-Up Night

You will need:

— invitations, either store-bought or homemade
— something nice for each person to wear
— a fresh corsage or boutonniere for each person
— a simple but elegant meal, if you plan to have dinner, or a special dessert
— a camera and film

We always seem to save our best for "company"—our best dishes, our best behavior, and our best clothes. Just for fun, plan a dress-up night at home!

The fun part of this event, suitable for any day, is that when family members put on their "best," their attitudes and behaviors reflect it!

Give everyone in your family a few days warning about "dress-up" night, because sometimes the anticipation of the event is more fun than the event itself! Write an invitation for each person, to read something like this: "You are invited to an elegant evening of good times and good food. Please dress in your best attire. The festivities will begin at 7:00 P.M."

Purchase or make a corsage or boutonniere for each "guest." (Some grocery stores have a floral department that sells these at a very reasonable price.) Although it is a simple thing, a corsage or boutonniere for a young child is a very special treat.

If you have young children, help them select their clothes and get dressed. If your children are older, let everyone plan his or her outfit and surprise each other at the party.

When the guests arrive, help them pin on their flowers. Comment on how nice they look, then spend a few minutes in conversation before asking them to join you for a meal or dessert. Be sure to take a family photo of this event!

19. Color-Coded Scavenger Hunt

You will need:

— a bag, basket, or box for each person
— a variety of colored items around the house or outside
— rainbow popsicles (optional)

Have fun hunting for special things together!

There are many different ways to play this game, but here are two suggestions to get you started. You might want to think of others to try on another day.

1. Each person looks for various items of different colors. The scavenger hunt is not over until each person's bag has many different items of all the colors of the rainbow.

2. Each person is assigned a color to hunt for. For example, a person assigned the color red looks for as many red objects as he or she can find that will fit in the bag and then returns to the "starting place" to compare objects with everyone else.

End your celebration of colors with a reminder of the promise God made when the first rainbow appeared in the sky. Then let everyone eat a rainbow popsicle to finish on a sweet note!

20. When Someone Is Sick

You will need:

— fresh or dried flowers
— a paper or cloth lace doily
— ribbon or yarn
— a rubber band

When someone in your family is sick, make this celebratory nosegay to leave on his or her pillow to show how much you care.

Gather the flowers into a small nosegay and fasten with a rubber band. Wrap the lace doily around the stems and tie a piece of ribbon or yarn into a bow. Lay the completed nosegay on the pillow of the person who is sick, perhaps with a note that says, "Hope you feel better soon!"

21. Refrigerator Riddles

You will need:

— your refrigerator
— magnets or tape
— paper
— pens or markers

Family Fun

Use your refrigerator, one of the most central places in most homes, as a place for solving riddles and learning new information.

Write a joke or riddle of the day on a card and post it on the refrigerator in the morning with a magnet or tape. Let everyone write an answer or response on a piece of paper and put it on the refrigerator near your card. Compare the answers at the end of the day and see who is right!

Or write a "question of the day" about science, a Bible story, or another subject on a piece of paper and post it on your refrigerator. Then write the correct answer on another piece of paper and put it into a sealed envelope. Add balloons, small pieces of confetti, and rolled streamers to the envelope, if you like. Place paper and markers nearby for everyone to write an answer to the question. At the end of the day, read all the answers together. Then open the envelope and read the correct answer. If anyone has answered the question correctly, throw the confetti on him or her and blow up the balloons to celebrate. This person can then be the one to determine what the next "question of the day" will be.

If no one has answered the question correctly, find the answer together (perhaps in the encyclopedia) and then celebrate with the confetti and balloons.

22. Words, Words, Words

You will need:

— a favorite refrigerator cookie dough recipe, or cookie dough from the refrigerator case of your grocery store
— baking equipment, such as a baking sheet, knife, etc.

Words of praise or encouragement always seem to make a day go better, especially when the words are spelled out in cookie dough!

Prepare your baking sheet as suggested in your cookie recipe or on the package of cookie dough. Cut slices of cookie dough into rounds; then roll the rounds into long "snake like" strips. Form the dough strips into the letters needed for your word or message and lay them on the baking sheet. Bake as directed.

When cool, arrange the cookie words on a plate for the whole family to see when they come to a meal. Or package the cookie letters and add them to lunch boxes for a mystery word to unscramble. (Be sure to give a clue or two about the word or first letter!)

Some words you might want to try: Super, Great, Wow, Fantastic, Wonderful, Excellent.

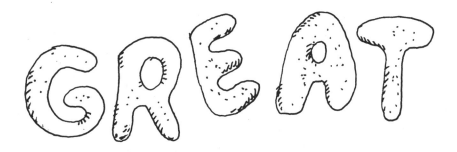

23. Backyard Cookout

You will need:

— a grill and other outdoor cooking supplies
— your favorite cookout foods

You don't have to wait for your next backwoods camping trip to have a cookout. Plan a cookout in your own back-yard, perhaps during the winter when most people wouldn't even think of it!

Get the grill ready and then prepare your favorite outdoor foods, such as hamburgers, corn on the cob (available all year in the freezer case of your grocery store), and ice cream. Have fun cooking and eating! If it gets too cold to eat out-side, take your cookout cookery indoors, spread a blanket on the floor, and turn the meal into an indoor picnic.

24. Stone Soup

You will need:

— a large cooking pot or crockpot
— a smooth, clean stone
— soup stock and other ingredients to make vegetable soup, such as potatoes, carrots, onions, seasonings, and so on
— a picture book that tells the story of Stone Soup (optional)

The story of Stone Soup has been passed down from gen-eration to generation in many different countries around the world. As the story goes, a traveler passing through a town is extremely hungry, but no one is willing to share anything to eat. So he convinces them that he has a magic stone that will make the most delicious soup in the world—and all you add to the cooking pot is water!

Of course, the people are curious to taste this soup and beg him to make it. So he puts his magic stone in a large pot of cooking water. "But the soup would taste much better with a few potatoes," he says. When a farmer hurries to add the potatoes, the traveler then says that the soup would taste even better with a few carrots. And so the story continues, with everyone adding an ingredient or two to make a delicious soup!

Tell the story of Stone Soup before making your very own soup. When you begin, make sure to wash the "magic" stone very well in hot soapy water; then add it to the cooking pot with the water. Let everyone participate in cleaning and cutting up the vegetables and adding them to the pot. As everyone is working together, celebrate the spirit of cooperation required to make this soup.

When your soup is done, carefully take out the stone and clean it for another day's use. Eat your hot soup with warm bread and butter!

25. Celebrating Our Ethnic Background(s)

Because we live in a global society, families have to work harder to retain their ethnic and cultural identities. If there are traditional celebrations from your ethnic background(s) that are not usually acknowledged by others around you, make these celebrations the basis for your own special family days. Or better yet, make them the basis for "any day" celebrations.

For instance, if there is a special breakfast bread that you remember from your childhood, why not search out the recipe for this bread and make it part of your family breakfast one morning a week? Can you set the table with special cloths that are also a part of that heritage, or are there unique dishes to use at that time that are part of your own growing-up years?

You also might recall prayers that your parents and grandparents taught you, as well as stories from your ethnic background(s). Sharing these stories and prayers, as well as old family photos, will help keep your family's roots alive for everyone in your family.

26. My Funniest Moment

Being able to laugh at yourself is a gift. Though it can be intimidating to recount your most embarrassing or funniest recollection when you are in a group of people you don't know well, the sharing of these memories isn't half as bad when you are in the midst of your family. In fact, it can be a cause for laughter!

Sometime when your family is gathered together, begin by asking everyone to think about the most embarrassing moment or the funniest thing that ever happened to each of them. Even though everyone may have heard these stories in some form or another before, the retelling bonds a family closer each time the stories are retold. As family members retell their stories, the laughter itself will be a celebration!

27. Getting to Know You

You will need:

— index cards, pens, and dice
  OR
— Life Stories™ game

Spend some time getting to know your family better, and have fun, too!

If you have the game Life Stories™ (available at a local toy or game store), play it according to the gameboard instructions. If not, have everyone in your family write one or more things he or she would like to know about the other family members on an index card. For example, "What is your favorite vegetable?" or "I think the hardest thing for me to do is . . . ."

Place the cards face down in the center of the table and take turns rolling the dice. The person who rolls the highest number draws the first card. After that person answers the question on the card, each person in turn answers the question. Play continues around the circle, with each person taking a card in turn and all family members answering the question. Of course, allow time for discussion of the questions you find most interesting.

Save your question cards for use at another time. This game can be expanded with new questions and played again and again.

28. Color Day

You will need:

— clothing of relatively the same color for each person
— ribbons or streamers of the same color
— foods or drink of that color, if possible

Sometimes when a family has a picture taken or goes on a trip, all the members wear the same color shirts to symbolize their family unity. Make a color day a regular any day celebration for your family.

In the morning, have everyone dress in the same color, or at least the same color shirt. Tie colored streamers or ribbons on the doorknob of your front door, and serve your meals with as many foods of that color as possible.

29. Knock-Knock Contest

You will need:

— a book of knock-knock jokes or other riddles

Jokes and riddles have their place in families! In fact, it seems to be quite a breakthrough when young children actually begin to understand how to tell a joke and what the punch line is. Knock-knock jokes are usually the first jokes that young children can begin to understand and repeat.

Your family might want to write your own book of knock-knock jokes and riddles! It seems that once you begin telling these jokes, they multiply.

Begin with simple, well-known knock-knock jokes; then encourage everyone to think up his or her own jokes. If you want, you can help by pointing out how words are similar to each other and how a word said "sloppily" can sound like another.

To have a contest, keep track of how many knock-knock jokes each person can create. Of course, the real prize is the fun and laughter as you celebrate your silliness!

30. Tongue-Twister Tournament

You will need:

— a watch with a second hand, or a stopwatch

A tongue-twister tournament is another twist (no pun intended!) on celebrating silliness!

The object of this game is to repeat a tongue twister as many times as you can without making a mistake. Time each person with a stopwatch and keep track of the scores. Repeat a new tongue twister each round, keeping score for that round. The person who wins the most rounds is the overall winner.

You may already know some tongue twisters, but here are some familiar ones to begin with:

Toy boat

Red leather, yellow leather

She sells seashells by the seashore.

Six thick thistle sticks

How much wood would a woodchuck chuck if a woodchuck could chuck wood?

If Peter Piper picked a peck of pickled peppers, how many pickled peppers did Peter Piper pick?

31. Funny Pizza Faces

You will need:

— one English-muffin half for each face
— tomato sauce
— thinly sliced or shredded cheese
— assorted pizza toppings, such as pepperoni slices, green pepper slices, olives, tomatoes, onion
— baking utensils

Funny faces can brighten up any day! Make edible funny faces to perk up everyone for lunchtime or a snack.

Let everyone create his or her own funny pizza face using an English-muffin half as the base. Spread tomato sauce on the muffin; then add pizza toppings to create a face. Round pieces of pepperoni make great eyes, green pepper pieces can be eyebrows, and thin cheese slices can be eyelashes. A tomato slice makes a great smile!

When everyone has made a face, admire the work and toast the faces in a 350-degree oven for about 7-10 minutes, or until the cheese melts and turns lightly brown. Eat and enjoy!

32. Backward Day

Plan a backward day, just for fun! This doesn't have to be an entire day of doing things backward, but just a few minutes of fun to make everyone laugh a little. What kind of things can you do backward? How about talking backward? Or dressing backward?

Have dinner instead of breakfast in the morning, and start with dessert. Set the table with the knife, fork, and spoon on opposite sides from their normal positions, and try sitting at the table backward!

When you read the paper, start at the last page and read toward the front.

The more things you try to do backward, the sillier you will feel. Have fun with this, even if it only lasts a few minutes—after that, frustration may set in for some people!

33. Sparklers

The next time fireworks are being sold in your area, usually in the early summer before the Fourth of July, stock up on sparklers. Some evening when it is dark and clear, take your family outside and light the sparklers. Try writing your names and other messages with the sparklers in the sky. Even though sparklers are usually the safest of all fireworks, be sure to keep a bucket of water nearby just in case.

34. Sock Slide

You will need:

— a variety of unmatched socks
— a paper or cloth bag
— an uncarpeted floor
— masking tape
— a small prize for the winner

Laundry day is a fun day to have a sock-slide contest. Place a variety of "mateless" socks in a special bag. Then let everyone choose two socks from the bag to wear in a sock-slide contest. Make start and finish lines on the floor with masking tape. Line up two contestants and have them take one or two steps, and then slide across the floor. The person closest to the finish line competes against the next contestant, and so on, until only two persons are left. The last slide determines the winner of the sock-slide competition! A prize could be a new pair of fancy socks.

35. Family Mailbox

You will need:

— a mailbox, or a box decorated to resemble a mailbox
— a good supply of envelopes, paper, and writing tools
— stickers, stamps, stamp pads, and other materials for decorating letters

Sometimes it is harder to communicate with those who live close to us, even those in our own households, than those who live far away. A family mailbox is a good way to help everyone keep track of one another's good and bad days, and it can be a source of daily celebration as well.

Set up the mailbox in a good location—somewhere everyone will be sure to check for mail each day.

Let family members write mail when they wish, using this system to keep track of schedule changes, to commend another on a job well done, to congratulate someone for completing a special project or scoring the winning goal in a soccer game, or to thank someone for the kind way he or she treats others. Using stickers and stamps to decorate the mail will make it even more fun.

36. Colorful Eggs

You will need:

— eggs
— an empty egg carton
— a saucepan and water
— an Easter-egg dye kit, or food coloring, vinegar, and water
— crayons or other materials for decorating the eggs

Why save colored hardboiled eggs just for the Easter basket? They can make any lunchbox festive, any day of the year.

Boil the eggs and let them cool. Prepare the egg dye according to the package directions, if you are using an

Easter-egg kit, or according to the directions on a food-coloring package, if you are using food coloring and vinegar. If you want to prepare the eggs for a dye resist, write a message on the eggs with crayons before dying the eggs. You could also tightly wrap rubber bands around the eggs or place stickers on them to make them dye resistant. Color the eggs in the dye, leaving them long enough to get a rich color. Set the eggs to dry in an upside-down egg carton.

37. Pancake Shapes and Messages

You will need:

— your favorite pancake batter
— a mixing bowl, spoons, spatula, and other cooking utensils
— a frying pan or griddle
— a clean, empty squeeze bottle, such as the kind that mustard or ketchup comes in

Pancake shapes and messages are a good start for any day! Mix up your favorite pancake batter and prepare your frying pan or griddle. Use a spoon or a squeeze bottle to create simple shapes or names and other words with the bat-

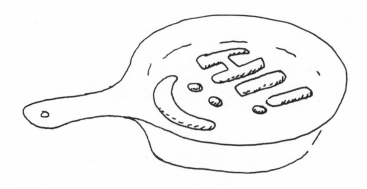

ter. A spoon works best for dropping the batter onto the frying pan or griddle to make bigger shapes. Favorite animals are also fun to make.

Serve these fun pancakes with your favorite pancake toppings.

38. Mug of the Day

You will need:

— a special mug (perhaps one that has a message such as "You are great!")
— a favorite hot drink, such as coffee, tea, or hot cocoa
— whipped cream, sprinkles, and other flavorful toppings
— a toothpick or beverage stirrer you have decorated with a flag that says, "You're great!"

Start someone's day right with a special hot drink. Rotate the honor of receiving the "mug of the day" to a different person each day, or give someone the "mug of the day" as an award or celebration on a special day. Prepare the person's favorite hot drink; then add a dollop of whipped cream, a few sprinkles, and a toothpick or beverage stirrer with a flag that says "You're great!" Greet the person with the special drink in the morning or at another time of the day.

39. A Bunch of Balloons

You will need:

— an assortment of balloons
— felt-tip pens or markers

Why do we always save balloons for birthdays and other special occasions? Balloons can make any day of the year fun!

Blow up a bunch of balloons and write messages on them, such as "WOW" or "You're fantastic!" Hang the balloons all around the house, or use them to decorate a person's bedroom door.

Another fun thing to do with a bunch of balloons is to fill the car with them on the morning of someone's birthday or another special day! What a surprise to wake up and find the car filled with balloons! If the balloons are for someone other than the car's owner or driver, be sure to add a message including the person's name. Also be sure there is plenty of time to remove all the balloons before it's time to go!

40. Home Sweet Home

You will need:

— one 16" x 20" piece of background material, such as muslin
— an assortment of scrap fabrics
— fusible web (available at fabric stores) or a good fabric glue
— embroidery thread
— assorted buttons and trims
— glue and scissors
— a picture frame to fit your finished sampler

Although the saying "Home Sweet Home" is a sentimental one, most people would have to agree that it feels good to be at home. Here is an idea for a no-sew home sampler that everyone in the family can make in celebration of home.

Cut about thirty squares from fabric pieces for a border, making each piece about 2" square. Cut one piece about 3" x 4" to represent your house, and cut appropriate sizes from other fabrics to make the windows, door, and chimney. You also might want to cut a small red heart to fit inside the roof, if you have red fabric. Other pieces you might want to cut include a tree, a fence, a sun, and other items that are in your own yard or the yard of your dream home.

Arrange the pieces on the muslin and attach them with fusible web or fabric glue. Arrange the border pieces around the outside and attach them as well. Add embroidery stitches to the shapes, if you like, or glue on buttons or other trims.

You can write the words "Home Sweet Home" with a marker on the sampler, making the letters look like tiny sewing stitches, or someone can embroider the letters on the sampler.

Hang your completed sampler where everyone who enters your home can enjoy it!

41. Paper-Bag Piñata

You will need:

— a paper bag
— paper scraps
— glue
— crayons or felt-tip pens
— string
— small surprises to go into the piñata, such as little toys or candies
— a small plastic baseball bat or a yardstick
— a blindfold

A piñata is a Mexican game that is fun to play together! Usually a piñata is made of papîer maché and takes many days to make, but you can easily make one from a paper bag.

Decorate the outside of the paper bag by drawing designs or adding paper cutouts to make it look like an animal, bird, or fish. Sometimes a piñata looks like the sun or a star.

After you have designed your piñata, fill it with the goodies you have collected. Tie the bag shut with string and hang it from the ceiling in your house or from a tree branch outside. Blindfold each person in turn, give the person a bat or yardstick, and then spin the person around three times. Point the person in the direction of the piñata and let him or her try to hit it with three swings. Whoever hits the piñata will hear the bag break. That's when the scramble begins to collect the goodies that have fallen out!

Variation: Fill the piñata with pieces of paper listing the chores that need to be done before a fun family outing is to take place. Write one chore on each piece of paper, such as "Take out the trash." Once the piñata is broken, everyone scrambles to pick up a piece of paper to find out what his or her chore will be. When the chores are done, you are ready to go!

42. A Special Heart

You will need:

— cake mix to make one two-layer cake
— one round and one square cake pan, of comparable size
— cake plate

Why save a heart cake just for Valentine's Day? It is easy to make a heart-shaped cake for any day you want someone to know how special he or she is to you.

Bake the cake as directed, using both the round and square cake pans. When the cakes have cooled, place the

square one on a cake plate and turn it so that it is diamond-shaped. Then cut the round cake in half and place each half against one top edge of the diamond. Now you have a heart-shaped cake!

Decorate the cake and serve it as a special any-day cake.

43. A Kiss for You

You will need:

— a funnel
— butter or margarine
— your favorite recipe for Rice Krispie bars, fudge, or popcorn balls, and the necessary ingredients and equipment
—plastic wrap and aluminum foil
—ribbon

Oversized candy kisses are fun to share with everyone in your family, whether as a special snack at home or a lunch-box surprise.

Grease the funnel, which will serve as the mold for your oversized kiss. Prepare your favorite recipe and pack it into the funnel. Pat it down at the bottom and then "pop-out" the kiss onto a piece of plastic wrap. Let cool a moment; then wrap in foil and tie with a bow.

The number of kisses you can make will depend on the size of your recipe and the size of your funnel. Be sure to lightly grease the funnel each time.

44. Family Totem Pole

You will need:

— boxes and other containers of all sizes
— paint
— construction paper and paper scraps
— felt-tip pens
— glue or tape
— glue gun

A totem pole tells a story about the history of a Native American family or tribe, or about an event of great significance in their lives. Make your own family totem pole to reflect your life together.

Experiment with stacking the boxes and other containers to make a totem-pole shape. When you are pleased with the configuration, paint or cover the boxes with paper. Tell stories by adding individual details to each of the boxes and containers with paint, felt-tip pens, or paper scraps.

Glue the boxes and containers together using a glue gun. When the family totem pole is complete, talk about what each part of the pole represents.

Variation: Design each portion of the pole to represent one member of the family, so that the completed totem pole reflects each family member and his or her unique contribution.

51

CELEBRATIONS
FOR YOUR OWN
SPECIAL DAYS

Celebrations for Your Own Special Days

Life in a family is full of special days—some more recognized than others. It seems that whenever an activity, event, or day is treated in a special way, it becomes more memorable and more significant. The ideas in this section are intended to inspire you to create more of your own special days.

45. Family Flag

You will need:

— a dowel, about 4 feet long
— fabric, at least 1 yard square for the background
— assorted fabric pieces or fabric paints
— scissors, glue, or Velcro
— sewing machine and sewing supplies

Some family names have a family crest or symbol. Even so, *your* family is unique. Let everyone in the family take part in helping design your own special flag.

Talk about the things that make your family unique, and incorporate those ideas in your flag. Use fabric pieces or fabric paints to decorate a fabric background. Sew a casing into the flag so that it can be mounted on a dowel. Hang the flag outside your home whenever someone in your family has a special day—or just because you want to remind everyone that you have a great family. (You also might want to create a special flag for each holiday of the year.)

46. Garage Door Billboard

You will need:

— a garage door
— tape and scissors
— large sheets of butcher paper and paints and brushes, or construction paper
— enlarged family photos (optional)

Renting a billboard is a wonderful way to announce a special message, but it is extremely costly. Make your own family billboard to highlight special days or events for your family, using your garage door as the base!

If you plan to use paint, cover the door with large sections of butcher paper. Paint a message on the paper, such as "Welcome home!" or "Do you know what is special about today?" If you plan to use paper only, cut the letters of your message out of construction paper and tape them to the door, along with a favorite family photo or two that have been "blown up" for the billboard.

This is a fun thing to do when someone in your family is celebrating a significant birthday or other special event.

47. Car Decorations

You will need:

— ribbon, crepe-paper streamers, or other decorations
— balloons
— posterboard and felt-tip pens

For many people, much of the day seems to be spent in the car as they commute to and from work, school, or other activities. Celebrate a special day by decorating your car appropriately.

Whatever you do, make sure that you do nothing to hin-

der the driver or obstruct vision. Plan your decoration theme according to the events of the chosen day. For example, if your family are fans of a particular sports team and that team is playing a game that day, you might want to decorate your car with your team's colors.

Banners and streamers can be wrapped around a radio antennae (make sure they are fastened securely so that they don't come loose). A pennant shape is easy to make from posterboard and can be attached to the car doors. Balloons can be tied inside the car, as long as they do not obstruct the driver's vision. In addition to these few ideas, you can purchase all kinds of items to stick to the insides of car windows. Be creative!

48. Kid's Day

You will need:

— a day that you have designated Kid's Day
— planned activities (see below)

We already know that there is Mother's Day and Father's Day. There probably isn't a kid around who hasn't wondered why there isn't an official Kid's Day. Of course, parents usually reply that every day is Kid's Day! Why not start your own Kid's Day to celebrate the gift of the kids in your life?

Begin the day with something fun for kids, such as breakfast in bed or a trip to a local fast-food restaurant that serves breakfast. If you have an entire day, plan a fun activity for everyone, such as a trip to the beach or the zoo. If you have your Kid's Day on a school day, be sure to send a special treat in the lunchbox, plan a festive meal for dinnertime, and make a card to thank your child for "just being you."

49. Apple Harvest

You will need:

— an apple orchard, or a market or grocery
— an apple press, apple corer, and other tools for various apple activities (see below)
— ingredients for preparing your favorite apple treats

Even if you and your family don't live in an agricultural setting, you can enjoy harvest time!

There are a number of different ways to participate in the apple harvest. Many communities have at least one orchard that allows people to pick their own apples. These orchards usually offer apple cider and other apple products for sale, and many have an apple press for making your own apple cider.

Visit an apple orchard and pick your own apples, or buy apples from a grocery store or market. Then use the apples to make apple pie, apple sauce, apple cider, apple prints (cut an apple in two, press one half into paint, and then print onto paper or a sweatshirt), or dried apple slices for eating or for making an apple wreath. You also can plant the apple seeds to see if you can grow a small apple tree of your own!

50. Saturday Silly Supper

You will need:

— favorite foods that you don't usually eat for supper, such as popcorn, breakfast foods, or the makings for ice-cream sundaes

Everyone needs a break, even the chief cook in your house! A Saturday Silly Supper is a meal where "silly" things are eaten—silly in the sense that you don't usually eat them for supper, such as popcorn and peanuts or ice-cream sundaes! Setting your "table" on the floor picnic-style is also a break from routine and makes the meal extra special. Sometimes just relaxing your usual supper routine will encourage family members to talk more freely and share their thoughts with everyone in the family.

51. Celebration Travel Sacks

You will need:

— paper or fabric bags
— assorted small items, such as paper and pencils, small travel games, puppets, little cars or toy dinosaurs, a cassette tape, books
— small packages of food, preferably nonsticky, including gum
— a damp cloth or small packets of prepackaged wipes

When planning a car trip with your family, it is important to plan for the inevitable boredom that long stretches of roadway can bring. Plan ahead by preparing celebration travel sacks. Even a relatively short trip will be eagerly anticipated when celebration travel sacks are in the car!

Pack the sacks with an assortment of items appropriate

for the ages of the occupants. Be sure to include a sack for each family member, including the adults in the car. A book on cassette tape, or a new or favorite music tape is a fun addition to any trip. Include a book of car games for added fun. A special touch: Add noisemakers and party hats to wear the last few miles of the trip!

52. Special-Day Tablecloth

You will need:

— a cloth tablecloth, preferably white or another light color
— fabric pens, or paints and brushes
— pencils

As family mealtimes become less and less regular for your busy family, begin a celebration tradition that can be used on any day, and especially on special days your family recognizes. A special-day tablecloth is fun to make and keep, adding to it event after event.

Have family members use pencils to write their names and special messages, trace their handprints (be sure to write the date beside each handprint), or draw pictures of the event on the tablecloth. Trace over the pencil marks with fabric pens or paints. Let dry, then place in a hot dryer for about ten minutes.

As you add to this tablecloth from special day to special day, your family will be able to recall past celebrations with pleasure!

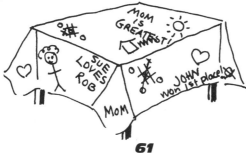

53. Anniversary Celebration

You will need:

— photos, slides, or a videotape of your wedding
— other memorabilia, such as brochures from places visited during the wedding trip
— a nice table setting and meal to share (see below)

Kids enjoy hearing stories about the past, especially stories about their parents' first encounter, courtship, and wedding. Include the whole family in an anniversary celebration of reminiscing!

Gather everyone together on an anniversary date to talk about your first encounter, your courtship and wedding, and your newlywed days. After telling the story of how you first met, show pictures from that time period. It's fun as you discover that your spouse remembers details totally different from the way you do! Look through the wedding photo album and show a videotape or slides of the wedding day, if you have them. Point out the relatives and friends who participated in the wedding and note how different everyone looks today. Then share a meal like your wedding meal, or one that is similar to the first meal you shared together in your new home. You might even want to purchase a small wedding cake from a bakery to share with your family!

54. Anniversary Ceremony

You will need:

— a simple bouquet
— your wedding rings
— a Bible
— a copy of your wedding vows
— rice or confetti

— tape recorder and cassette tape, or video recorder and videotape

Any wedding anniversary is a fun time to let your children reenact the wedding, playing the parts with you. Very young children really enjoy doing this!

Choose the parts of the ceremony that your children will play, with one child acting as the minister, another as the maid of honor or best man, and another as the one to "give" the bride away. Of course, you will need to vary the roles according to the number of children you have.

Begin the ceremony with special music, either from your wedding or current music that you like. Form an aisle and have a child escort the bride, or let the bride and groom walk together to meet the minister. It helps if the child playing the minister can read the wedding vows and Bible verses you chose, but this is not essential. A very young child can memorize a few short lines. After the exchanging of vows, the minister pronounces the couple husband and wife and everyone throws rice or confetti. Be sure to record the ceremony on cassette tape or videotape and add it to your other wedding mementos.

55. Cake of the Day

You will need:

— ingredients and equipment to bake a cake
— frosting and decorating tools

Cakes aren't just for birthdays! You can make a cake in honor of an event, activity, or person, any day of the year. Here are some ideas for making cakes to make the end of mealtime extra special.

Soccer-Ball Cake: Bake two round cakes. When cool, layer them. Referring to a soccer ball, use white and dark chocolate frosting to duplicate the ball design on the cake top. You can decorate cakes as other sports balls, too, for the times when someone has taken up a new sport or won a championship.

Hamburger Cake: Bake two round cakes. When cool, layer them. Use several colors of frosting to decorate the cake like a hamburger: light chocolate for the bun, dark chocolate for the hamburger patty, green for the lettuce, and red for the tomato. This is a great cake to serve when someone in your family has just started work at the local fast-food restaurant!

Of course, you can buy many different kinds of cake molds and pans, but it is always fun to create your own special cakes, using your own designs.

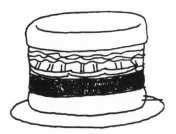 

56. Time for a Time Change

You will need:

— new batteries for smoke detectors, alarm systems, clock radios, and other battery-operated appliances
— an egg timer
— all the clocks in your home
— a large sheet of paper and paints, or felt-tip pens
— a pizza or other fast-food meal to bake in the oven

When it is time to change your clocks again, make it a celebration!

Make a banner to hang over the doorway to announce the celebration, perhaps using the words, "Do you know what time is it?" or "Time's-a-changing!" If you have children who don't understand why we have a time change, you might want to explain the reason for daylight saving time.

Set your timer and pop a pizza or other fast-food dish into your oven for the designated cooking time. Then have everyone in the family go from room to room and try to reset all the clocks before the oven timer goes off. Enjoy dinner when you are through.

57. Report-Card Day

You will need:

— beverage glasses
— sparkling cider, seltzer water, or another favorite carbonated beverage
— a small gift for each person receiving a report card

Report-card day is important, not only for the person who is receiving the report, but also for everyone in the family. Celebrate with the students in your family by using one or more of these ideas.

Be ready for the student or students as they arrive home from school. After settling in and putting schoolbooks away, pour everyone a glass of something fizzy to drink and toast all the students for doing their best work.

After looking at all the report cards and noting any comments that teachers have made, offer congratulations or encouragement to the students and give each of them a special gift.

Some possible small gifts that would be appropriate for

all ages are a unique pair of socks, stationery, a stamp pad and stamp for embossing, colorful markers, or a special pen.

58. Red-Letter Day

You will need:

— a calendar
— a red crayon or marker
— other red things, including red foods such as strawberries, apples, or red-gelatin dessert
— red clothing items, a red tablecloth, or anything else red you can use to signal that it is a red-letter day

We sometimes talk about a day being a "red-letter day," but not everyone knows what that means. Just for fun, plan a red-letter day for your own family that can be celebrated periodically.

On a day of your choosing, set the breakfast table with a red cloth or red placemats, and/or wear a bright red shirt. Announce to your family that "This is a red-letter day!" and explain that a red-letter day is a day on which something special happens. If nothing special is planned for that day, suggest that thinking positively about the day will help everyone see the good in all that takes place that day.

Mark your family calendar with a red X in the day's square, or color the entire square red to help you remember it. At the end of the day, you might want to serve one or two red foods as a reminder of the red-letter events of the day. Talk about these events and list them on the calendar.

59. A Leafy Maze

You will need:

— fallen leaves
— rakes

Finding your way through a maze is always fun—and sometimes challenging! A leaf maze is a fun fall activity for all ages.

Use rakes to form fallen leaves into piles in the yard and then "scoop" the piles of leaves into a maze formation. You might want to have your maze lead from the driveway, through the front yard, and around to the front door; or you might want to extend the maze to side or back yards as well. Of course, this will depend greatly on the amount of leaves in your yard!

Try different ways of getting through the maze—walking, running, skipping, and hopping, to name just a few. Have fun!

60. Follow the Clues

You will need:

— 3″ × 5″ index cards
— pens
— string or yarn
— balloons

Everyone loves a treasure hunt, and it is especially fun to have a treasure hunt on a day when a fun event is planned!

When you have surprise tickets for a sporting event, movie, or play, plan a treasure hunt for members of the family to find the tickets.

If you have very young children, run a length of yarn or string along your planned path, pulling the string through keyholes, under doorways, and around corners. End with the tickets tied to a balloon with a string.

If you have older children who can read, write clues leading to your hiding places on index cards and hide the cards along the path. Begin by giving them the first card and then watch them go! The more creative you are in writing the clues, such as using rhymes and riddles, the more fun it will be. Tie balloons to the end prize—the tickets or other surprise.

61. It's a Puzzle

You will need:

— jigsaw puzzle
— a large sheet of posterboard or other heavy paper
— felt-tip pens or markers and pencil
— scissors and glue

Here's another fun way to announce a surprise family excursion or special-day outing. Trace any jigsaw puzzle pattern onto a sheet of posterboard. Before cutting the puzzle pieces apart, write a message, draw a picture, or glue a brochure onto the pieces to reveal the excursion or outing that you have planned.

After you cut out the pieces, put them in a basket and let everyone put the puzzle together to discover what fun you have planned!

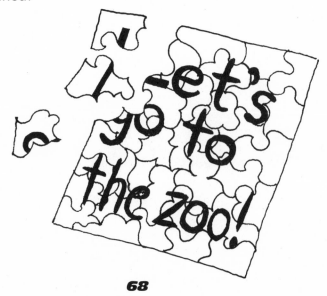

62. First Day

The first day of every season of the year is special, as we read in Ecclesiastes—"For everything there is a season" (3:1). Make each "first day" extra special by trying some of these ideas as a family affair!

Fall: Eat a lettuce leaf salad. Run through a pile of leaves. Polish your boots. Make a centerpiece with pumpkins, gourds, and squashes. Bake pumpkin muffins. Drink apple cider.

Winter: Make snow cones with shaved or crushed ice. Clean the freezer! Bake cookies to eat with hot cocoa—don't forget the marshmallows on top. Buy a new pair of knitted gloves or mittens for each person in the family, have everyone put them on, and take a group picture with everyone waving.

Spring: Bring a branch into the house and "force" it into bloom by putting it into a bucket of warm water by a sunny window. Wash your windows. Hang a wind sock outside your window. Go fly a kite!

Summer: Go wading at the beach or in a park fountain. Plan a picnic in the park. Take a family picture beside—or in—a swimming pool. Buy new inexpensive plastic sandals for everyone and decorate them with paints or glue fake jewels on them. Play a game of baseball.

CELEBRATIONS FOR SPECIAL PEOPLE

Celebrations for Special People

Everyone deserves to feel special—at least for a day! It is easy to remember to treat family members extra nice on a day such as their birthday, but it is even more meaningful to treat them well on another day of the year. Here are some ideas to help you make someone feel appreciated and loved any day of the year, as well as on a birthday or other special occasion.

63. Your Special Day

As you look through a calendar, notice all the days that are celebrated—from traditional holidays such as Christmas and Valentine's Day to days such as Sweetest Day and Secretaries' Day. Designate one day a month to honor one of the people in your family, other than an already established special day. Mark each chosen day on the calendar with a person's name and let other family members know ahead of time so that they can help you plan the festivities. Some of the things you might like to do include cooking the person's favorite meal or taking him or her to a favorite restaurant, planning a trip to a place the person has always wanted to go, or buying a balloon bouquet to present to the person at school, work, or home.

Half of the fun of this day is the planning that goes into it. Because it is a day that you and your family have picked, it may turn out to be even more fun than a holiday or birthday!

64. Crown of the Day

You will need:

— thin cardboard
— gold or silver spray paint
— "fake" jewels purchased from a craft store, or cut from
  construction paper
— glue, stapler, scissors, and tape

We all have days when we feel that everything is going our way—and days when everything seems to be going from bad to worse. Keep a crown in the cupboard for those moments when someone needs to feel extra special.

Cut a crown shape from thin cardboard and spray with gold or silver spray paint. When the paint dries, glue on fake jewels or paper jewels cut from construction paper to make a regal design. Staple the ends of the crown together, or cut a slit in one end of the crown so that the other end can slide through. This way the crown can fit everyone in the family on his or her day.

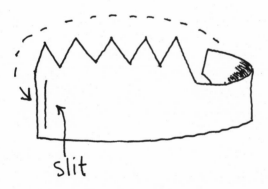

slit

65. King or Queen for a Day

You will need:

— a chair to use as a throne
— a crown (see p. 74 or purchase a crown from a party store)
— a robe
— a box or bag of prizes, such as coupons to a fast-food restaurant, parking passes, new pencils with the person's name imprinted, and other fun but inexpensive items

There used to be a television show called "Queen for a Day." If you were chosen as Queen for a day, you wore the robe and crown and sat on the throne while the host of the show showered you with gifts and prizes. Every once in a while, why not designate your own king or queen for a day?

Plan the "ceremony" for a day when everyone in the family can attend. Have the designated person sit on the throne while you place the crown and robe on him or her. Let each person think of one or two compliments to give to the royal person; then allow the king or queen to make a wish or two (within reason!) for things other family members can do. This might include such things as clean his or her room, vacuum out the car, play a board game, dust the house, or walk the dog. Then give the royal person the day off from any chores around the house and let him or her open and enjoy the gifts!

66. New Baby in the Family

There are many ways to celebrate the birth of a new baby in the family. Here are just a few ideas to get you started—you'll probably think of many more!

Plant a Tree: Purchase a tree that is in bloom the month the baby is born and plant it somewhere in your yard. Every year when the tree blooms, you will be reminded of the birth of the baby. In some countries, people plant an apple tree for the birth of a boy and a pear tree for a girl.

Balloon Bouquet: Once the new baby arrives, buy a balloon bouquet—pink for a girl, blue for a boy—and tie it to your front-door handle or your mailbox. This way you can share this exciting day with the entire neighborhood!

Kite Flying: In Japan, it is customary to fly a kite upon the birth of a new baby. Usually, a fish kite is flown from the rooftop on the day of a baby boy's birth; another animal on the day of a baby girl's birth.

Time Capsule: When a new baby is born, collect the newspaper from that day, a weekly news magazine from that week, and other items that are representative of that time. Place the items in a box, including the baby's photo, and mark it to be opened every year on that date.

67. Celebrate Family Pets

You will need:

— an appropriate pet treat for each pet
— blue ribbon and a juice can lid for each pet
— scissors and glue
— permanent felt-tip pen
— a camera and film

Plan a day to celebrate the pets in your family!

To make each pet a medal, measure and cut a length of blue ribbon to fit around the pet's neck—or around a fish bowl or cage, if your pet cannot wear a ribbon around its neck! Then glue a juice can lid to the ends of the ribbon, forming a loop. Use a permanent felt-tip pen to write your pet's name and "1st Place" on the lid.

If your pet can do tricks, have a pet show and award him or her with a pet treat and the ribbon medal. Be sure to take a picture of the happy pet!

68. Plate of the Day

You will need:

— a glass plate
— paint or pens made especially for painting on glass (available at a craft store)

You can purchase a red plate that has the words "You are special today" printed all around the edge. If you don't already have a plate like this, you might want to purchase one to use when serving someone deserving special recognition. Or you can make your own special plate of the day.

Follow the directions on the paint or paint pens to decorate your plate with the words "You are special today," or something else that will be significant for your family. Finish the plate as directed by the paint instructions. Enjoy!

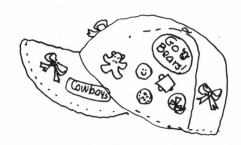

69. Hat of the Day

You will need:

— a simple straw hat or other hat that can be worn by men or women
— ribbons, small trinkets or charms, and other decorations
— a glue gun

In years past, people wore hats for every special occasion. In fact, a holiday or special occasion was often the time when someone purchased or made a new hat. Create a family hat that can be worn by each family member whenever it is his or her special day.

For starters, add a hatband made of ribbon, fastening it to the hat with a glue gun. Then add a trinket or decoration or two to the brim or band of the hat.

As the hat is worn by family members, let each person add a symbol of his or her day to the hat. For example, when a child's team wins a soccer tournament, add a button with the team's name to the hat. Or if Mom or Dad wins $25.00 in a radio call-in contest, glue two or three play dollar bills to the hat. Throughout the year, family members will be able to retell their important moments by looking at the hat of the day!

70. Fly a Banner

You will need:

— a flagpole
— a roll or large sheet of sturdy paper
— scissors, colorful markers, and staples or tape

Sometime you might want to let everyone know how you feel about someone. How creative can you be?

If you can find a company in your area that will fly banners behind an airplane, it is fun to do so! But just as much fun is to fly your own banner from the rooftop of your house or garage.

Make a large banner from sturdy paper, print the message you want to share in large letters across the banner, and attach it to a dowel or long pole with staples or tape. On the designated day, fly your banner from the rooftop for everyone to see. (A flag pole will work for this as well.)

You might want to fly a banner for family members on graduation day, promotion day, report-card day, or any day—just because you love them!

71. Illuminated Homecoming

You will need:

— paper bags, such as lunchbags
— sand or aquarium gravel
— one votive candle for each bag
— paper hole-punch or scissors

When someone in your family is arriving home from a trip or special event after it is dark, use luminaries to make the homecoming special!

If you want to, cut or punch a design in the paper bags so that the candlelight will shine through. Experiment with folding the bags so that you can punch both sides at the

same time. Pour a shallow layer of sand or gravel in the bag; then set the candle in it. Be sure to open the bag fully and place the candle in the center, so that there is no danger of the bag catching on fire. If it is a little breezy, you might want to reconsider using luminaries on this evening.

Line the luminaries along the pathway to your home and light the candles a few minutes before you expect the person to arrive. What a fun way to come home! Luminaries are also fun to use when camping (as long as there is no fire danger) or when you are hosting a family reunion or party.

72. Homecoming Festivities

You will need:

— a large "WELCOME HOME" banner
— decorations such as balloons and streamers
— a football or other ball to play a family homecoming game, or a board game that your family would enjoy
— favorite foods and drinks to share (perhaps the honoree's favorite meal)

When a family member is returning home after being away for an extended length of time, such as returning from summer camp or a school trip, plan your own family homecoming.

Hang a "WELCOME HOME" banner on a garage door or the front of your house, and add any other decorations that you would like. Arrange to have everyone in the family on hand when the "guest of honor" arrives home and greet him or her with music or a loud cheer. After exchanging stories about the trip and family events, share the meal or special foods you have prepared and play a family game. (Depending on the game you choose, you may want to play the game first.) Be sure to post the winning score!

73. Roadside Message

You will need:

— permission to post a series of temporary small signs along a roadway
— posterboard or cardboard
— posts and a staple gun or string
— paints or felt-tip pens
— string

There was a time when Burma Shave signs lined the highways and byways. A portion of a message was printed on each sign. After passing the last sign in the series, you had the complete message.

Make someone special feel great by greeting him or her with a series of signs along the route to home. Write your message, perhaps only one or two words per sign, making sure that the beginning of the message is what the person driving, riding, or walking home will see first.

After receiving permission to post your message in someone's yard, do so along the edge. Or tie the signs to utility poles along the way, making sure that you take down all the signs by the end of the day.

74. Give Me a Smile

You will need:

— a camera
— foods that shouldn't be eaten while wearing braces

Having braces on your teeth can be a traumatic time, regardless of age. Even though the end results are wonderful, sometimes the process is not a very pleasant experience. Make the day that the braces come off a celebration for everyone to participate in!

On the night before the braces are taken off, take a photo of the person wearing his or her biggest smile. The next day, after the braces have been taken off, take a picture of the person wearing his or her biggest smile ever!

Serve a dinner of all the things that the person didn't eat—or shouldn't have eaten—while wearing braces—such as corn on the cob, caramel bars, bubble gum, and other crunchy or sticky snacks.

75. Losing the First Tooth

Losing the first tooth is a significant day in the life of any child. And it is significant for the parents as they realize their child is growing up. Here are some ways to celebrate this rite of passage. If you don't subscribe to the myth of the Tooth Fairy in your home, you can adapt these ideas to suit your needs.

Tooth Pillow: Make or purchase a small pillow and sew a small pocket to the front of the pillow to hold the lost tooth. You can add gold tassels, braid, and other designs to the pillow to make it special. Place the tooth in the pocket and leave the pillow with a note to the Tooth Fairy beside the bed at night.

You might want to write this note to the Tooth Fairy: "In this pocket you will find, a teeny, tiny tooth of mine. So while I sleep where dreams are made, let's see if we can make a trade!"

Before and After Photos: When your child has a loose or wiggly tooth, be sure to take a picture of him or her wearing a big smile. Then take another picture the day after the tooth comes out. Add these photos to your family photo album.

For Good Care of Teeth: Make the loss of that first tooth a significant one. Plan a trip to the drugstore and purchase a brand new toothbrush, tube of toothpaste, and dental floss to celebrate the loss of the tooth. Use this opportunity to reinforce the importance of taking good care of your teeth for a lifetime.

Super Sippers: One of the fun things about losing a tooth is the "window" that it makes in your mouth! Cut a tooth shape out of construction paper and make two slits in the tooth as shown. Then slip a straw through the super sipper and let the toothless person sip milk or juice through a straw at mealtime!

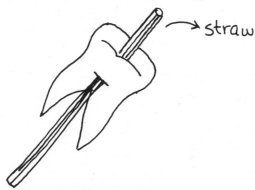

straw

76. A New Driver in the Family

You will need:

— a neighborhood or city map
— highlighter pens
— signs or posters, balloons, streamers, and other decorations

The day there is a new driver in the family is significant for many reasons! The entire family can enjoy celebrating this special event.

Use a highlighter to trace a familiar route on a map of your town or neighborhood. For example, you might trace a route that passes by the local school, your church, a neighborhood market or grocery store, and winds up at your family's favorite pizza or ice cream parlor. Along the route, place signs or posters that you have decorated with messages, such as "You made it!" or "Another safe driver is on the road!" Add balloons and streamers to the signs and post the signs in the ground with stakes. (Be sure to go back at the end of the day and remove all of the signs you have posted.)

Gather the family in the car. Give the map to the designated "navigator" and have the navigator sit in the front seat with the new driver. You can make this a mystery trip, if you like, not telling the driver where you plan to end up! Follow the route, making sure that the new driver notices the signs you have posted along the way. End your first trip with the new driver with a pizza dinner or an ice-cream cone for dessert.

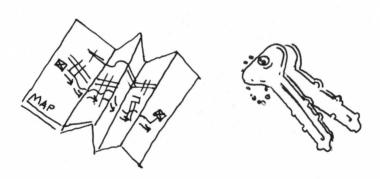

77. Star of the Week

You will need:

— a bulletin board or other display space
— photos, awards, and other items that symbolize the person of the week's interests, hobbies, and achievements

Sometimes a teacher will highlight a student of the week in the classroom. At that time, the student brings in photos, awards, and other items that symbolize his or her interests, perhaps placing all of the items on a bulletin board for everyone to see.

Even though you live with your family, you and your family may not know everything about one another. If you have a "star of the week" display once in awhile, you just might be surprised what you learn!

Your bulletin board may be a cork board that you have prepared, or it may be the front of the refrigerator. It won't matter, once you post a sign at the top that says "Star of the Week." Arrange the display items in a pleasing fashion on the board and enjoy celebrating the person you are highlighting!

78. Birthday Predictions

You will need:

— paper and pens for each person
— a notebook for each person

Give a new type of gift for birthdays this year—birthday predictions for the coming year!

Label each notebook with the person's name and birth date. Then, a few days before the birthday, give everyone a sheet of paper and pen to write down wishes, hopes, and dreams for the birthday person. On the birthday, have everyone read his or her "predictions" for the birthday person; then place them in the notebook, where they can be read and reread throughout the coming year. It is fun to keep these letters from year to year and see how you grow and change.

79. Award of the Week

You will need:

— certificates you have purchased (from an office-supply store) or made (some computer software programs do this)
— gold-seal stickers

Why do we always wait for someone else to acknowledge the people in our family for their good work and achievements? Make weekly awards a fun part of your family life!

Keep a supply of certificates and gold-seal stickers in a drawer where everyone in the family can use them. You might want to start with such predictable awards as bringing home a great report card, getting a promotion, or winning a chess tournament. Other things are fun to give awards for too—preparing a great new recipe, going a week without biting your nails, remembering to do your chores, or doing something nice for someone else.

You can present the award of the week any time, but it is fun to make a big deal of it by presenting the award with everyone in attendance—so that they can applaud the recipient.

80. An Envelope of Wishes

You will need:

— a colorful envelope
— colorful pens, glue, glitter, or stickers to decorate the envelope
— notepaper or slips of paper

If someone in your family has had a disappointment, or is anticipating a special event or a new venture, create a surprise envelope of good wishes to start his or her day!

Decorate an envelope, which can be used again and again, by writing "Words for the Day" on it with colorful pens; or write the words with glue and then sprinkle glitter over them. On a piece of notepaper or on individual slips of paper, write words of encouragement and Bible verses that are reminders of God's loving kindness. Slip the paper(s) into the envelope and leave it where the person will see it in the morning—perhaps on the breakfast table or inside a backpack or briefcase.

81. A Candy Lei

You will need:

— fresh or silk flowers
— thin twine, thread, or string
— gum or candy

A lei is a Hawaiian necklace made of flowers and worn for special occasions. In Hawaii, it is a sign of honor and welcome to place a lei around the neck of an arriving guest. You can make flower or candy leis to honor one or more family members on a special day.

It is easy to make a lei by threading twine or thread through the centers of the flowers as shown. Or you can make a lei of gum and candy by punching a small hole in the center of each piece and then threading the twine or thread through the hole. Because the heavier pieces of candy will fall together, you may want to tie knots between the pieces to help keep them an even distance apart.

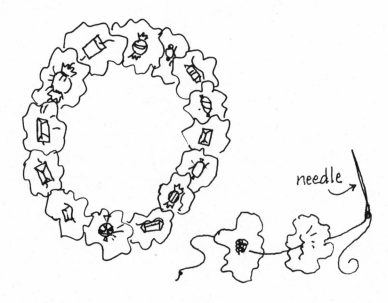

needle

82. Family Portrait Gallery

You will need:

— a blank wall in your home
— a variety of picture frames, including collage-type frames that hold several pictures
— photos
— scissors

Many homes have a family portrait gallery—a wall of photos that usually includes school photos of the children, family photos, and perhaps photos from past generations too. If you don't already have one, you might want to create a wall like this in your home, where you can celebrate all the people in your family—past, present and future!

Sorting through your family photos together is a good way to recall important people, places, and events in your family's history. As you do this, set aside your favorite photos to use in your photo gallery.

If you have some photos in which one or more people look great, but another person has his or her eyes closed, use scissors to cut these photos apart and fit the pictures into collage-type frames. Frame other photos as you wish. Then arrange all the frames on your wall to make your photo gallery.

You might want to take time periodically to rearrange and replace some photos with new ones or others that you like. Even though these photos may stay on your wall a long time, you will be amazed by how many people will examine them again and again, and in doing so, will see something they haven't noticed before.

83. Placemat of Honor

You will need:

— a gold-star placemat
  OR
— shiny gold paper, or posterboard and gold spray paint
— scissors
— self-adhesive paper (optional)

With today's more casual lifestyle, people use placemats on their tables more often than tablecloths. A placemat of honor is a good way to celebrate someone's special day.

Purchase or make a gold-star placemat. If you are making the placemat, cut a star shape from shiny gold paper. Or cut a star from posterboard, spray paint it gold, and let it dry. Laminate the star shape (this can be done at many educational stores, as well as some office-supply stores), or cover the star with clear self-adhesive paper.

On a day that is special for one member of your family, affirm that you believe he or she is a "star" by placing the placemat under the person's breakfast cereal bowl. It will surely STAR-t the day off right!

84. Your Light Shines

You will need:

— a candle
— matches

Jesus reminded us to let our light so shine before others that they might come to know God. We need to remember that all our gifts, talents, and abilities come from God and that through us, other people can come to know and love God. Honor the times when family members share their light with others!

Keep a candle on a table or in a front window. When someone in your family shares his or her light with others, light the candle as a reminder that all of us are called to share the light of Christ.

85. Crown of Flowers

You will need:

— fresh flowers
— needle and thread
— ribbons
— wire (optional)

Make a crown of fresh flowers to celebrate someone in your life.

As soon as you pick or purchase the flowers, sew them together with a needle and thread to make a crown. If you like, gently wrap the flowers around a wire. Attach ribbons to hang from the back of the crown.

86. Broom Person

You will need:

— a broom
— felt pieces and yarn
— hats and other clothing items
— large wiggly eyes (available from a craft store)
— glue gun and stapler
— poster board and markers

Let the neighborhood know when someone in your family has done something deserving recognition by making a broom person to put in the yard!

Turn the broom so that the handle is pointing down. Glue wiggly eyes onto the bristles with a hot glue gun; then glue on felt pieces to make a mouth, nose, and other features. Add yarn hair, a hat, and other clothing items, if you wish.

Make a sign to announce the special event—such as "Shannon turns 10 today!"—and glue or staple this sign to the broom handle. You may want to shorten the broom handle before pushing it into the ground in your front yard for the neighborhood to see.

87. Cook of the Day

You will need:

—favorite recipes and cookbooks
—recipe ingredients and cooking utensils
—a chef-style apron (one that you have purchased or made of white cloth or muslin)
—fabric paints (optional)

It seems that knowing how to cook is becoming a lost art in our world of frozen foods and fast-food restaurants. Yet time spent preparing and sharing a meal can be the most significant and memorable of family times. Try this idea to help each family member feel important, as well as to teach your children how to cook and share cooking responsibilities in your home.

Personalize a chef's apron that can be worn by the cook of the day. You might want to use a favorite slogan, such as

"Kiss the Cook" or something else that has meaning for your family. Or you might want everyone in your family to write his or her name on the apron. First write on the apron; then paint over the writing with fabric paints.

Let the cook of the day choose the recipes and take the lead in preparing one or more meals for the day. Of course, young children will need adult supervision and assistance, and older children will enjoy delegating tasks to other family members.

If Cook of the Day becomes a favorite family activity, start a notebook or recipe file of favorite recipes for easy use when repeating a meal.

88. The Sunshine Award

You will need:

— a "happy face" or sunshine pin or button
  OR
— posterboard, markers, and a safety pin

Some groups give a "sunshine" award to the person with the best attitude. Families can do the same! Use this award idea to keep your family thinking positively.

Buy a "happy face" or sunshine pin or button, or make one using posterboard, markers, and a safety pin.

Explain to your family that having a good attitude is something that doesn't just happen. Sometimes it takes a little work to keep a positive attitude. Show them the sunshine pin or button, and pin it on the person you think has had the best attitude during the day. Then inform that person that he or she is to pass the button to the person who has the best attitude the next day, and so on, so that each day someone receives the button for having the most positive attitude.

CELEBRATIONS FOR HOLIDAYS

Celebrations for Holidays

I t's often easy to get pulled into the commercial aspects of holidays—from Christmas to the Fourth of July—or to get into a holiday rut by never trying any new celebrations. In this section are some simple and fun ways to celebrate holidays with your family. Most likely, you will find many of them to be new and different. Add them to the ways your family already celebrates the holidays, or use them as springboards for thinking of other creative ideas.

89. New Year's Day (January 1)

Every country around the world has special celebrations for the first day of the new year. If your family has traditional celebrations, by all means, continue them! If not, here are a few suggestions that your family might want to try.

Money for Others

You will need:

— small envelopes
— several dollar bills or shiny quarters

For the Chinese New Year celebrations, special "lucky money" is put into red envelopes and given to everyone. Why not adapt this idea to the story Jesus told of the three servants (Matthew 25:14-29)?

Retell the story of the servants to your family; then give each person an envelope with several dollars or shiny quarters in it. Encourage them to think about how they might increase their money and offer its return in a charitable way. Help one another throughout the year, and celebrate the many ways that you can help others.

New Year's Cake

You will need:

— one silver dollar wrapped in foil
— a favorite family cake and candles

A New Year's cake is a welcome part of the celebration for many families. Bake a favorite family cake. Wrap a silver dollar in foil and put it in the cake batter before baking. Add enough birthday candles to the cake to celebrate the number of years that you have been a family—a great way for all families, especially a blended family, to show unity and family love. As you blow out the candles, make a family "wish" and offer your wish to God in a short prayer. Let the person who has the piece with the silver dollar in it choose a game or other fun activity you can enjoy together!

Family Photos

You will need:

— photos taken during the previous year
— empty photo albums and envelopes

Many families enjoy a day of watching football on New Year's Day. For those family members who would enjoy an activity to keep their hands busy and help pass the time, why not place all the photos taken during the past year in photo albums? Put any duplicates or pictures of other people into envelopes and make plans to deliver them to relatives and friends in the coming weeks.

90. Groundhog Day (February 2)

You will need:

— several bright lights and a blank wall
— white paper, pencils, scissors, and tape
— black paper, or paint and paintbrushes

What better way to celebrate Groundhog Day than by having a shadow party? Ask family members to bring their shadows with them! Shine a few bright lights in the room so that you can make shadow hand puppets on the wall.

You also can make silhouettes by taping a sheet of white paper to a wall and shining a bright light on the paper. Then have someone sit between the light and the wall and let someone else trace the person's silhouette on the paper. Cut out the silhouette and trace around the shape on black paper—or paint inside the silhouette with black paint.

91. Valentine's Day (February 14)

Valentine's Day is a good time to celebrate the love within a family. Although most family celebrations are expressions of our love for one another, the hearts we see in abundance on Valentine's Day are symbolic reminders of this love. Here are a couple of Valentine's Day celebrations the whole family can enjoy.

Heart Muffins

You will need:

— your favorite muffin recipe and ingredients
— a muffin tin and other baking equipment
— marbles or small balls of aluminum foil

Make heart-shaped breakfast muffins. If you don't have a heart-shaped muffin pan, fill a regular muffin tin with paper muffin cups and place a marble or small ball of aluminum foil between each muffin cup and the muffin tin. This indentation will make the muffin form a heart as it bakes.

Heart Walk

You will need:

— walking shoes for each person

You can celebrate Valentine's Day all month long by making February "heart walk" month. Because walking is good exercise for the heart, it is an ideal activity for every family member. While you are walking, pick up any trash and aluminum cans you find along the road. Walking will be good for you, and picking up the trash will be good for the environment. Donate the money you collect from recycling the aluminum cans to a charity of your choice—perhaps the American Heart Association!

92. Random Acts of Kindness Day (February 17)

You will need:

— a box
— items to send to persons in need: combs, shampoo, toothbrushes, toothpaste, pencils, books, socks, etc.

Random Acts of Kindness Day is a relatively new holiday, but one that many people have practiced daily for years. Designating a day for kindness helps people make a conscious effort to be sensitive to the feelings and needs of others. Remind your family members that though it is good to do special deeds for others on special days, it is also important to practice small acts of kindness each and every day.

On this special day, make a friendship box to share your kindness with persons in your own community or around the world. Contact your local Red Cross or the Red Cross National Headquarters (American Red Cross National Headquarters, International/Youth Services, Attention: Friendship Boxes, Washington, DC 20006) and ask for suggestions of items needed by persons in a particular city, state, or county. Most likely, your family will be able to choose where you would like your box to be sent. It will feel great, knowing that you have shared your kindness with others around the corner or around the world.

93. St. Patrick's Day (March 17)

You will need:

— paper, pencil, scissors, and tape
— thin cardboard
— frosted cake (preferably white frosting)
— green sugar crystals

The story of St. Patrick's Day is a good story to know. Even though the typical decorations for St. Patrick's Day are shamrocks and little green leprechauns, the meaning of St. Patrick's Day has its roots in the Christian tradition. Take a trip to your local library and let the children participate in "researching" the history of St. Patrick's Day.

If your children are ready for abstract concepts, tell them that the three leaves of the shamrock can symbolize the Trinity—the Father, Son, and Holy Spirit—and talk briefly about the Trinity. Then make a shamrock to use in decorating the top of a special dessert.

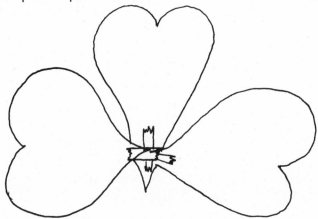

First, cut out three heart shapes and tape them together at the points (see diagram above). Then trace around your shamrock pattern on thin cardboard, cut out the cardboard shamrock, and press it into the top of a frosted cake (white frosting is suggested). Lift off the cardboard shamrock and sprinkle green sugar crystals into the shamrock shape. Enjoy!

94. April Fool's Day (April 1)

April Fool's Day is well known as a day for tricks! Of course, it's fun to set someone's clock ahead, substitute salt for sugar in the sugar bowl, and play other fun tricks. Having a "backward" dinner is also fun. Begin with dessert, use unusual eating utensils, turn the chairs around backward, and so forth.

95. Easter Day (see calendar)

You will need:

— candy and other small treats
— cereal bowls and Shredded Wheat cereal
  OR
— shoes and artificial Easter grass

Surprise each family member on Easter morning with a different type of Easter basket. Leave a "nest" in each family member's cereal bowl or shoe. For a cereal bowl nest, use Shredded Wheat as the nesting material; then fill the nest with small treats. For a shoe nest, line the shoe with artificial Easter grass and fill it with candy and other goodies.

96. Arbor Day (April 24)

You will need:

— a tree for planting
— a shovel and other tools for planting a tree
— camera, film, and photo album or scrapbook

Arbor Day is a holiday without as much fanfare as the others, but an important one just the same. On Arbor Day, it is traditional to plant a tree—a good way to celebrate the life of your family! Choose a favorite fruit or flowering tree, or a tree that your family admires, and plant it in your yard. As the years pass and your tree grows, keep a photo "growth chart" of your tree through the seasons. Record how much the tree has grown beside each photo, along with special memories or events from the season.

97. May Day (May 1)

You will need:

— construction paper or decorative paper
— scissors, tape, and stapler
— flowers, cookies, lollipops, or other treats

Celebrate May Day with May Day baskets. To make each basket, roll a piece of construction paper or decorative paper into a cone shape, tape the edges, and staple a paper strip to the top of the cone for a handle. Fill the baskets with flowers, cookies, lollipops, or other treats, and hang a basket on the doorknob of everyone's bedroom.

You might want to make May Day baskets to share with others who live in your neighborhood or apartment building.

98. Flag Day (June 14)

You will need:

— at least one flag to fly outside your home
— a small flag for each family member
— a recording of patriotic music
— red, white, and blue crepe paper streamers, balloons, or other decorative items

Make Flag Day a day for your family to honor your country. Decorate your front door with red, white, and blue decorations. If you don't have a flag-pole holder, install one so that you can hang your flag early in the morning. Have family members look in an encyclopedia to find flag facts (such as when the first American flag was flown, how many stars and stripes it had, etc.) and proper flag etiquette (such as when to fly a flag, how to hang it and fold it, etc.). Then give everyone a small flag to wave as you play patriotic music.

99. Independence Day (United States—July 4; Canada—October 10)

You will need:

— a flag of your country
— fireworks or firecrackers, if they are legal in your area
— sparkling punch or soda
— drinking glasses
— straws

The day of independence for any country is a day to remember and celebrate. Those of us who live in freedom can never truly understand how difficult it is to live in a country where the simplest freedoms have been taken away.

Plan your Independence Day celebration with your entire family. If you don't already have a flag of your country and a place to display it, this might be your first activity. If you are planning on having a fireworks display, you will want to save your celebration until it is dark. At that time, pour sparkling punch into glasses, toast your freedom, and light the fireworks.

As you are enjoying the spectacular lights, reflect together on how many choices and opportunities you have because of the generations before you who fought for their freedom—and yours. If you can, retell the story of how freedom came to your country and say a prayer in honor of the men and women who died for that freedom.

100. Friendship Day (August 6)

You will need:

— cards and envelopes (commercial cards or cards made with paper, felt pens, and other materials)
— a large piece of paper
— felt-tip pens
— photos of each family member, or a photo of your entire family

The date on the calendar for Friendship Day is August 6, but you can celebrate Friendship Day any day of the year. In fact, if more people "celebrated" Friendship Day every day, the world just might be a happier place!

Write the words "A friend is . . ." on a large sheet of paper and hang it on your refrigerator or somewhere family members will see it. Leave enough space on the paper so that everyone can add a word or picture thoughts to finish the sentence. You might add a few words to the paper to get everyone started, such as *kind, loving, caring, helpful,* and so on.

After doing this, sit down together to make friendship cards for the friends in your lives. You can send cards to personal friends of each person, to teachers or other influential friends, as well as to entire families who are friends with your family. For a special touch, have each person include his or her picture in each card, a picture of your family, or an invitation to join your family for dinner or tea sometime.

101. Grandparents' Day (September 10)

You will need:

— newspaper or magazine clippings from the year(s) the grandparents were born or from significant years of their lives
— photos, advertisements, and music from the same years
— party decorations, such as crepe-paper streamers, balloons, and party hats

Invite the grandparents over to celebrate their special day, perhaps by making an invitation that has a photo or advertisement from the chosen years of the grandparents' lives on its cover. Print the words "Because you are you, we want to celebrate!" inside the card, and add pertinent details such as the date, time, and so on.

Plan the event, such as an afternoon tea or dinner. Allow time for asking questions about what life was like during the chosen time period, looking at old pictures and magazines or other memorabilia, and honoring the grandparents by naming the gifts and talents each person has received from them.

Of course, it is always fun to include music and dancing at a celebration. Perhaps you can convince the grandparents to teach you a few dance steps from their younger days!

Although the official Grandparents' Day is September 10, you can celebrate this day any time of year. Wouldn't it be fun to honor grandparents once a month?

102. All Saints Day (November 1)

You will need:

— a family Bible or other documents that list members of your family tree
— a branch or sturdy twig
— gold spray paint
— small gold picture frames, with a small loop at the top for hanging (available at craft and hobby stores)
— a container to put the twig in
— plaster of paris
— small family photos
— ribbons

All Saints is a day when Christians honor those who have lived before them by remembering the things they did and saying prayers of thanksgiving.

Many families keep a record of their ancestors in a Bible or on a chart that shows their family tree. This is called genealogy and is a hobby that many families take up together. You can find the family tree of Jesus and others in books of the Bible. These lists go all the way back to Adam and Eve!

Decorate a branch or sturdy twig with gold spray paint. When dry, place the twig in a container and fill the container with plaster of paris or some other material that will harden and hold the twig securely in place.

Then do a little research together to determine the family members you will display on your own family tree. Mount available photos of family members in small gold frames and arrange them on the tree in order, from youngest to oldest. For those family members without photos, put a frame in each one's "spot" and make a note to try to find a photo or other information to add to the frame later.

As you are working on this project over time, share the stories of these saints who lived before us, talk about how they have influenced our lives and the decisions we have made, and discuss how we can continue to share with others the good things we have learned from them.

Place your family tree where everyone who comes into your home can enjoy it. It will be quite a conversation piece!

103. Thanksgiving (Fourth Thursday in November)

You will need:

— an ear of Indian corn
— a small basket

There are many reasons to celebrate on Thanksgiving Day. The story of the first Thanksgiving is familiar to most people, but not everyone may know about Squanto's gift to the Pilgrims—the knowledge to grow corn in the New World.

Although we don't often eat Indian corn, it is a colorful addition to our Thanksgiving meal. As a special way of sharing thanks in your family, break off several kernels from an ear of Indian corn and place one beside each place setting. Sometime during your Thanksgiving meal, pass a small basket around the table and have family members name one thing they are thankful for as they drop their kernels into the basket.

Variation: Place a handful of kernels at each place setting and continue passing the basket around the table and naming blessings until all of the kernels have been dropped into the basket. Look how full your basket is at the end of your meal!

104. Christmas

Christmas is a favorite family holiday. There are entire books of ideas for things to make and do and ways for families to celebrate the birth of God's Son, Jesus.

Of course, the four weeks before Christmas, called Advent, are a time of great anticipation and excitement as we prepare for Christmas Eve and Christmas Day. Family members of all ages enjoy making cookies, making and wrapping presents, decorating the house and Christmas tree, and singing Christmas carols together.

It is a good idea to hang a family calendar in a prominent place and use it to keep track of all the parties, plans, and special events involving family members. This is a place where you can mark a special Christmas concert that the children are performing in, a day of family baking, and a day for a family outing to select and cut a Christmas tree. It is easy to make your own special calendar. Simply purchase a calendar and seasonal stickers; then attach the stickers to indicate special family days or events.

Many families today are combating the commercialization that seems to have taken over this sacred holiday by refocusing their Christmas energies on the true meaning of Christmas. Cutting down on the number of holiday events and expectations is a good way to begin.

Whatever your family pattern is for fun and celebration during the Christmas season, remember to take time to enjoy the gift of one another. After all, isn't the gift of love what the season is really all about?

105. New Year's Eve (December 31)

Recent research indicates that most people ring in the new year with a family party at home. Here are some fun things to do while you wait for the clock to strike midnight.

Party Masks

You will need:

— construction paper, paper and fabric scraps, sequins, feathers, and assorted trims
— glue, glitter, and scissors
— craft or popsicle sticks

Cut out a simple mask shape for each person and let everyone decorate a mask with glue, glitter, sequins, feathers, and any other assorted scrap materials that you have on hand. Be sure to cut eye holes in the masks and glue a stick to one back side of each mask for a handle. Use the masks to ring in the new year!

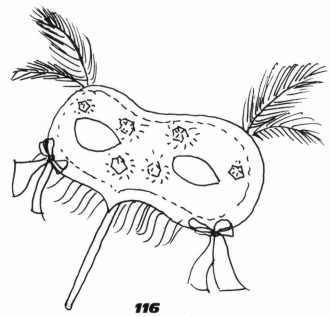

Crazy hats

You will need:

— paper plates or large sheets of paper
— paper and fabric scraps, glitter, sequins, and other trims you have collected
— glue, tape, and scissors

An alternative to making masks for New Year's Eve is making crazy hats to wear! Use either a paper plate or a large sheet of paper rolled into a cone for the base. Decorate the hats with paper and fabric scraps, as well as glitter, sequins, and other trims you have collected. Have a contest for the most creative hat, and give a prize to the winner. Let everyone wear his or her crazy hat as the clock strikes midnight!